ORGANIZE YOUR MIND

Clear Critical Thinking Systems And Models

Kevin Wagonfoot

CONTENTS

INTRODUCTION: SETTING THE STAGE FOR CLARITY AND PRODUCTIVITY

"With realization of one's own potential and self-confidence in one's ability, one can build a better world."

— DALAI LAMA

In today's fast-paced world, the onslaught of information and rapid changes can often leave us feeling overwhelmed and disoriented. In the midst of this chaos, the capacity to organize and harness one's thoughts emerges as a critical skill, offering not just relief but a pathway to success and fulfillment. We will look into the art of mental organization, revealing how a structured approach to thinking can elevate your productivity and propel you towards your aspirations. It's about turning the tangled web of thoughts into a strategic map, where each thought is not a barrier but a catalyst, propelling you forward. You'll discover practical strategies and insights that transform mental chaos into clarity and purpose, allowing you to navigate life's complexities with confidence and precision. Learn how to reshape the landscape of your mind, turning potential stumbling blocks into the stepping stones of a successful and organized life.

The Critical Role Of Clear, Organized Thinking

Success is not solely about having the right resources or connections; it hinges profoundly on our ability to think clearly and organize our thoughts effectively. The renowned author Joseph Murphy once noted, "Change your thoughts, and you can change your destiny." The foundation of personal achievement lies within the power of our thoughts. Organized thinking helps build a robust mental framework, which is crucial for tackling challenges and seizing opportunities with precision and confidence.

Mental Organization: A Pathway To

Enhanced Productivity

Mental organization isn't just about having an orderly mind; it's about aligning our cognitive processes to boost efficiency and effectiveness in our personal and professional lives. It's arranging our thoughts to reflect clarity, enabling us to focus better and accomplish tasks competently. We will explore various mental organization systems and models, providing a toolbox of strategies to refine your thought processes.

The Benefits Of A Structured Approach To Thinking

Adopting a structured approach to thinking and decision-making can transform how we handle our daily tasks. It minimizes time wasted on indecision and maximizes outcomes by enabling a more straightforward path to action. This approach enhances personal productivity and improves our ability to make sound decisions quickly and effectively.

What To Expect: Systems And Models

This book is broken into 5 parts, each containing several models and tools to help you organize your mind and thoughts.

Part I: Foundations of Mental Organization establishes the basic techniques for mental organization. We begin with *Mind Mapping*, a visual tool that enhances creativity and clarity when organizing thoughts. Following this, *The Eisenhower Box* introduces a time-management model that effectively prioritizes tasks. The section on *Meditative Practices* focuses on developing concentration and reducing cognitive load.

Part II: Advanced Cognitive Strategies This section introduces sophisticated strategies for refining mental processes. *Cognitive Restructuring* offers methods from cognitive-behavioral therapy to alter negative thinking patterns, enhancing emotional and mental clarity. *The Feynman Technique* presents a learning method that improves understanding and communication of complex information by teaching others.

Part III: Problem Solving and Decision Making Part III presents systems that enhance decision-making and problem-solving abilities. *The Five Whys* provides a simple iterative technique to identify the root cause of problems. *Lateral Thinking* includes strategies for innovative and outside-the-box thinking. *The Checklist Manifesto* highlights how checklists can prevent mistakes and ensure consistency in complex processes.

Part IV: Continuous Improvement and Learning This section is dedicated to methods for lifelong learning and continuous personal development. *Decision Fatigue* focuses on managing the exhaustion that comes from frequent decision-making. *The OODA Loop* offers a model for rapid decision-making and action in dynamic situations. *Meta-Cognition* covers higher-level thinking skills that enhance control over one's learning processes.

Part V: Integration and Application The final part of the book emphasizes integrating and applying the discussed techniques into daily routines for better mental organization. *Digital Detox* suggests benefits from periodically disconnecting from digital devices to reduce mental clutter. *The Art of Reflection* presents reflective practices that encourage learning from experiences. *Systems Thinking* shows how to manage complex systems with a holistic approach.

Each section builds on the previous, culminating in a comprehensive approach to enhancing mental clarity, productivity, and effectiveness in various aspects of life and work. By experimenting with these techniques, readers can discover the methods that best suit their needs, fostering a lifelong journey of learning and self-improvement.

Achieving More Through Applied Techniques

The promise of mental organization is in understanding its principles and applying them.

This book aims to equip you with the necessary skills to implement these techniques in various scenarios. You will have learned to effectively organize your thoughts to achieve clarity and productivity by the end. Moreover, you can tailor these strategies to fit your needs and lifestyle, enhancing personal growth and professional development.

The journey involves the discovery and practical application. The following chapters will expand on this groundwork, each dedicated to exploring a distinct tool or technique. We aim to inform and transform how you think about and manage your cognitive resources. By the end of this book, you will understand the importance of mental organization and possess the skills to master it, paving the way for a more productive and successful life.

If you are going to organize your mind its equally important to organize the space you inhabit. I have a special gift for you. I've written a helpful companion book, "**Organize Your Cleaning**," I'd love to share a complimentary copy with you. Just visit KevinWagonfoot.com, enter your email address, and the book is yours. Plus, by signing up, you'll receive my weekly newsletter covering various topics, from mental models and performance enhancements to practical tips for organizing your life.

Scan QR Code for free book download

PART I: FOUNDATIONS OF MENTAL ORGANIZATION

CHAPTER 1: THE FOUNDATION OF MIND MAPPING

"Creativity is just connecting things. When you ask creative people how they did something, they feel a little guilty because they didn't really do it, they just saw something."

- STEVE JOBS

Mind mapping is a dynamic tool that caters to the mind's inclination to think about associations and relationships. It serves as a graphical means to represent ideas and concepts, which helps organize information, make decisions, and enhance one's ability to remember details. We will examine mind mapping, trace its origins, and examine how it aids in various aspects of personal and professional life, such as project management, meeting preparation, and brainstorming.

Defining Mind Mapping

A mind map is a visual diagram that organizes information around a central concept, represented by an image at the center of a blank page. From this core idea, related thoughts and keywords extend in various directions, creating a network of nodes. Each branch features a key image or word along its line, with lines becoming thinner as they move away from the center. To enrich the diagram, colors, images, and symbols are frequently employed.

The mind map is more than just a mnemonic device; it mirrors the radiant associative thinking of the human brain, where each piece of information connects with another, leading to a sprawling web of associations. This makes it a potent tool for extracting and visualizing the connections that might be less obvious with linear thinking methods.

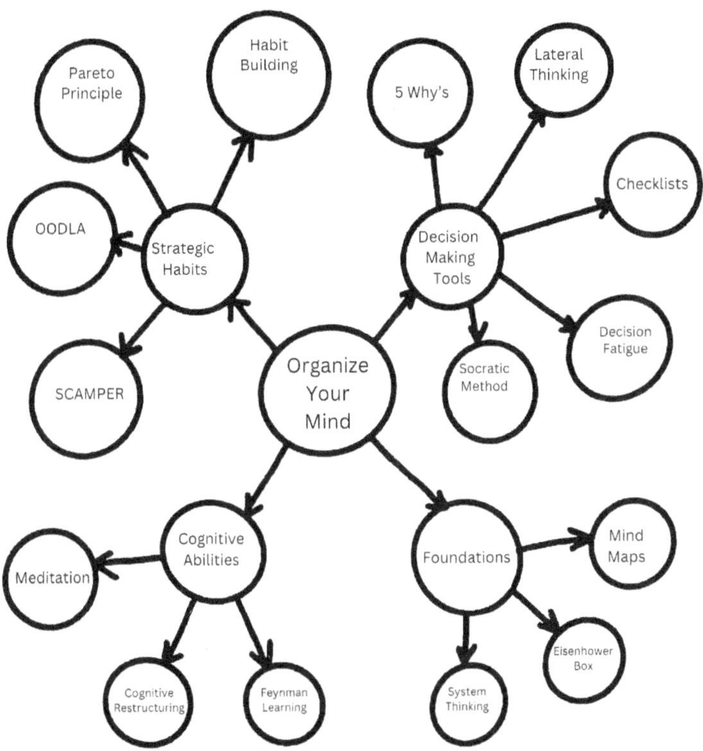

This is an early Mindmap I created while working on this book

Origins Of Mind Mapping

In the 1970s, Tony Buzan, an author and educational consultant specializing in psychology, brought widespread attention to the concept of mind mapping. Buzan drew inspiration from historical figures such as Leonardo da Vinci and Albert Einstein, who extensively used diagrams to articulate ideas and tackle problems. As formalized by Buzan, mind mapping taps into the brain's cortical skills—such as imagination, color perception, and spatial awareness—to stimulate creativity and make thought processes more cohesive and energetic.

Applications Of Mind Mapping

Project Management: Mind maps can dramatically improve project management by breaking complex projects into more manageable components. Each branch of a mind map can represent a different aspect of the project, such as resources, tasks, deadlines, and contingencies. This visual overview ensures that project managers and team members can see the relationship between different activities and better organize the workflow.

Meeting Preparation: Mind maps can streamline meeting preparation. They help structure agendas, note vital points to discuss, and assign action items. During the meeting, a mind map can also take live notes, categorize discussions, and make them easy to reference later.

Brainstorming: Mind maps are excellent for brainstorming because they encourage the free flow of ideas and help spark new thoughts through association. Mind maps facilitate a creative environment where participants can build on each other's ideas, whether used individually or in a group setting.

Creating Effective Mind Maps

Here are steps to guide you in creating a practical mind map:

Start in the Center: Use an image or text to represent the central idea you're exploring. This is usually done in landscape mode to allow the freedom to expand in all directions.

Use Colors Wisely: Colors can help separate different ideas or categories, provide visual stimulation, and make your map easier to memorize and review.

Incorporate Images: Images have the power to convey much more than words and help improve memory retention. They also make the mind map more engaging and fun to work on.

Connect Branches: Starting from the central image, draw branches outwards that represent significant categories related to the topic, and from these branches, draw smaller branches for related sub-topics.

Keep it Clear: Use single words or simple phrases to convey information clearly and effectively. This makes it easier to see the connections between different map elements.

Digital Tools For Mind Mapping

While traditional pen and paper work well for mind mapping, numerous digital tools enhance the experience by offering functionalities such as easy editing, collaboration features, and integration with other digital applications. Software like *XMind, MindMeister,* and *Microsoft Visio* provide robust platforms for creating detailed and aesthetically pleasing mind maps.

Mind mapping is a transformative tool that leverages the brain's natural penchant for synthesis and association. Whether you're a student, professional, or someone looking to enhance your creative and analytical skills, mind mapping offers a valuable framework for structuring thoughts, making complex decisions, and fostering innovative thinking. As we progress further into this book, the techniques outlined here will serve as a foundational skill set for developing more advanced cognitive and organizational capabilities.

CHAPTER 2: PRIORITIZE YOUR TASKS

"In preparing for battle I have always found that plans are useless, but planning is indispensable."

— DWIGHT D. EISENHOWER

In the quest for productivity and effective time management, distinguishing between what is urgent and what is essential becomes crucial. The Eisenhower Box, a straightforward yet effective tool for task prioritization, offers clarity in distinguishing important tasks. We will cover the Eisenhower Box, exploring its origins and demonstrating how it can enhance efficiency and decision-making in both personal and professional settings.

The Eisenhower Box

The Eisenhower Box, also known as the Eisenhower Matrix, is a task prioritization method that uses a four-quadrant box to help you decide on and manage the urgency and importance of your tasks. This method helps visualize the workload, enabling users to focus on functions critical to their success and well-being while either scheduling, delegating, or dropping less vital tasks.

Origins And Historical Context

Named after Dwight D. Eisenhower, the 34th President of the United States and a distinguished five-star General during World War II, the Eisenhower Box draws from Eisenhower's frequently cited insight: "I have two kinds of problems, the urgent and the important. The urgent are not important, and the important are never urgent." This guiding principle was a cornerstone in navigating the multifaceted challenges of his military campaigns, presidential duties, and personal affairs. Stephen Covey later brought this methodology to a broader audience in his book, "The 7 Habits of Highly Effective People," which highlighted the Eisenhower Box as an essential tool for effective time management and decision-making. Covey's endorsement helped cement the tool's relevance in both personal effectiveness and professional productivity, illustrating how strategic categorization of tasks can lead to more focused and deliberate action.

Understanding The Four Quadrants

Urgent and Important (Do First): These tasks require immediate attention and carry significant consequences if not completed. Examples include crises, deadlines, and urgent problems. Prioritizing these tasks helps in managing immediate pressures that demand attention.

Necessary but Not Urgent (Schedule): These tasks are essential for long-term success and should be planned later. Activities include relationships, planning, and recreation. Focusing here helps build a sustainable environment that enhances future performance and well-being.

Urgent but Not Important (Delegate): These tasks require immediate attention but contribute little to long-term objectives. Examples include calls, emails, and interruptions from others. Delegating these tasks can free up time for more significant pursuits.

Neither Urgent nor Important (Eliminate): These are the least productive tasks that can often be eliminated. Examples include time-wasters, leisure activities, or distractions that do not serve any personal or professional purpose. Removing these tasks can significantly increase productivity and save time for important tasks.

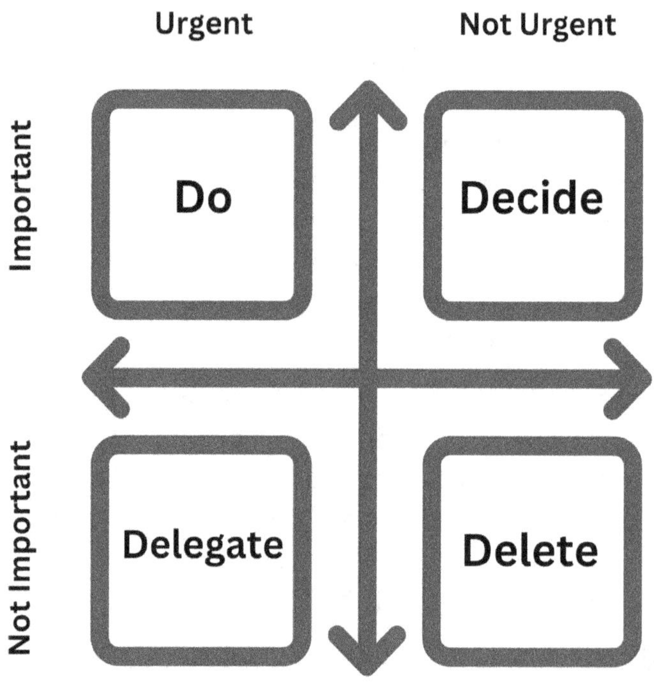

Simple example of an Eisenhower Box

Practical Applications

Daily Task Management: By categorizing tasks into one of the four quadrants, individuals can plan their day more effectively, ensuring that they focus on what truly matters. This prevents the common pitfall of spending too much time on urgent but ultimately unimportant tasks.

Project Planning: In project management, the Eisenhower Matrix can help identify tasks that should be prioritized or scheduled and those that should be delegated or dropped, ensuring efficient use of resources and time.

Team Collaboration: When used in a team setting, this matrix helps clarify roles and responsibilities, ensuring everyone is focused on the right tasks. It can also help identify areas where processes can be streamlined, or additional resources are necessary.

Tips For Implementing The Eisenhower Box

Regular Review: Tasks and priorities can change, so it's essential to review and reassess task categorization regularly.

Limit Tasks: Limit the number of tasks in the "Do First" quadrant to avoid overwhelm and ensure you are not mistaking important tasks as urgent.

Use Technology: Numerous apps and software tools are designed to help users utilize the Eisenhower Matrix more effectively. Tools like Trello, Asana, or the Eisenhower app can facilitate this method by allowing users to categorize and monitor tasks digitally.

Learn to Say No: Effective task management is knowing when to say no to tasks that fall into the "Urgent but Not Important" or "Neither Urgent nor Important" categories, especially if they interfere with your high-priority goals.

The Eisenhower Box is more than just a productivity tool; it is a mindset that emphasizes the importance of focusing on what actually adds value to your personal and professional life. By effectively categorizing tasks according to their urgency and importance, you can improve your efficiency and overall life satisfaction by focusing on tasks that align with your long-term goals and values. As we move forward in this book, the principles of the Eisenhower Box will recur, providing a foundational strategy for managing time, decisions, and priorities in various aspects of life.

PART II: ENHANCING COGNITIVE ABILITIES

CHAPTER 3: MEDITATIVE PRACTICES FOR FOCUS ENHANCEMENT

"If you are quiet enough, you will hear the flow of the universe. You will feel its rhythm. Go with this flow. Happiness lies ahead. Meditation is key."

— BUDDHA

In the ever-accelerating pace of modern life, our minds often scatter in multiple directions, diluting our ability to concentrate and maintain focus. Meditative practices counterbalance this trend, providing techniques that enhance mental clarity and focus. This chapter looks into the different types of meditation, their specific benefits for mental clarity, and practical guidance on integrating these practices into a busy schedule.

Overview Of Meditation And Its Benefits

Meditation is an ancient practice used to achieve a deep state of peace and mental clarity. While it originated in spiritual and religious traditions, today, meditation is recognized widely for its cognitive and physiological benefits. These benefits include reduced stress and anxiety, enhanced emotional health, improved attention span, and greater overall well-being.

Types Of Meditation For Focus Enhancement

Mindfulness Meditation: This form of meditation involves paying attention to thoughts, sounds, the sensations of breathing, or parts of the body, bringing your focus back whenever the mind starts to wander. Mindfulness helps cultivate awareness and presence, enhancing concentration and focus.

Guided Meditation: Often led by a narrator, guided meditation directs the practitioner through a series of mental images or scenarios that promote calmness and relaxation. It can benefit those requiring more structure in their meditation practice.

Transcendental Meditation: This technique involves silently repeating a personal mantra, such as a word, sound, or phrase, in a specific way. This form of meditation allows the individual to settle inward to a deep state of relaxation to achieve inner peace without concentration or effort.

Focused Attention Meditation: This technique sharpens the mind by focusing on a single object, sound, or visualization. The practice revolves around concentrating the attention on a particular object throughout the session, cultivating the ability to remain focused.

Breathing Techniques For Focus And Stress Reduction

Breathing techniques are pivotal in meditative practices, deeply affecting both mental and physical health with their simple yet profound mechanics. Among these, the 4-7-8 breathing method stands out for its simplicity and effectiveness. Developed by Dr. Andrew Weil, a pioneer in integrative medicine, the 4-7-8 technique draws from ancient yoga breathing principles known as *pranayama*, which aim to regulate the breath to enhance life force or *prana*.

The 4-7-8 breathing method involves a structured

pattern where you breathe in quietly through your nose for four seconds, hold the breath for seven seconds, and then exhale forcefully through the mouth for eight seconds, making a 'whoosh' sound. This specific rhythmic pattern is not arbitrary; it is designed to bring about a state of deep relaxation and has roots in the centuries-old yogic practice that helps control the body's response to stress.

The 4-7-8 breathing technique is particularly useful for managing stress and anxiety. By altering the breath cycle, the method helps to slow the heart rate and encourage the body to take up more oxygen with each breath, which is key in activating the parasympathetic nervous system—the body's natural relaxation response. This can make it an invaluable tool in preparing for stressful situations, improving emotional regulation, and transitioning smoothly into sleep.

Its benefits extend to aiding individuals in coping with insomnia. The technique's ability to relax the mind and body sets a conducive stage for sleep, making it easier to fall asleep and potentially increasing the quality of rest. As a relaxation aid, it can also be beneficial before or after engaging in high-stress activities or to calm the mind before critical tasks that require deep concentration.

Physiologically, the 4-7-8 technique works by influencing the body's autonomic nervous system. The extended exhalation in relation to inhalation reverses the respiratory pattern that occurs naturally under stress, which often involves quick, shallow breaths. This shift helps to decrease the fight-or-flight response of the sympathetic nervous system, enhancing a state of calm. By spending more time on exhalation, the body is forced to slow down, focusing inwardly and calming both the mind and body.

The method's emphasis on rhythm and repetition also aids in mental focus, pulling attention away from stressors and redirecting it towards the count and sequence of breathing. This act of focusing can by itself be a meditative practice that many find therapeutic.

Integrating the 4-7-8 breathing technique into daily routines can be a simple yet powerful way to harness the body's natural ability to relax and rejuvenate, offering a readily-accessible tool to enhance mental clarity and manage stress effectively.

Integrating Meditation Into A Busy Schedule

One of the common barriers to meditation is the perceived need for more time. However, meditative practices can be highly flexible and require as little as five minutes. Here are some tips for incorporating meditation into a busy lifestyle:

Start Small: Begin with just five minutes in the morning or evening. Gradually increase the time as you become more comfortable with the practice.

Use Breaks Wisely: Take breaks during the workday to practice breathing exercises or mindfulness. Even a few minutes can reset your mental state.

Be Consistent: Try to meditate at the same time every day to establish a routine that becomes a regular part of your life.

Use Apps and Online Resources: Numerous apps provide guided meditations, timers, and tips to help you practice effectively, even on the go.

Addressing Common Challenges And Misconceptions

Meditation can seem daunting despite its benefits due to common misconceptions such as the need for perfect calm, hours of dedication, or religious affiliation. It's important to understand that meditation is a personal experience and can be tailored to fit individual needs and lifestyles. Additionally, the mind wandering during meditation is natural and part of understanding your mental habits.

Meditative practices offer valuable tools for enhancing focus, reducing stress, and improving decision-making capabilities. By adding these practices into your daily routine, you can develop a sharper, more present mind that can better handle the complexities of modern life. As we continue to explore cognitive and organizational strategies throughout this book, the techniques discussed in this chapter will serve as essential components in the toolkit for achieving mental clarity and productivity.

CHAPTER 4: REWIRE YOUR THOUGHT PROCESSES

"Beliefs have the power to create and the power to destroy. Human beings have the awesome ability to take any experience of their lives and create a meaning that disempowers them or one that can literally save their lives."

— TONY ROBBINS

Cognitive restructuring is a core technique in cognitive-behavioral therapy (CBT) that aims to help individuals recognize, challenge, and alter stress-inducing thought patterns. We will discuss the significance of cognitive restructuring, outlines the step-by-step process involved, and illustrates its role in managing stress, enhancing decision-making, and boosting overall mental wellness.

Understanding Cognitive Restructuring

Cognitive restructuring is based on the idea that distressing emotions and maladaptive behaviors stem from mental processes. Individuals can develop more balanced and rational thoughts by identifying and adjusting these cognitive distortions or irrational thought patterns, leading to healthier emotions and behaviors.

In the realm of CBT, cognitive restructuring is vital for addressing a variety of psychological issues, including anxiety, depression, and phobias. It empowers individuals to take control of their thoughts, which often dictate emotional responses, thereby reducing symptoms of psychological distress.

Step-By-Step Guide To Cognitive Restructuring

Identification of Negative Thoughts: The first step involves becoming aware of problematic thought patterns. This often requires monitoring one's thoughts and emotions to recognize triggers that provoke cognitive distortions.

Analysis of These Thoughts: Once identified, these thoughts must be challenged. This involves questioning their validity and the evidence supporting these beliefs. Critical questions might include, "Is this thought based on facts or feelings?" and "What evidence supports or contradicts this thought?"

Development of Rational Alternatives: The next step is formulating more balanced and rational responses after challenging these thoughts. This doesn't mean replacing negative thoughts with overly positive ones but finding truthful and balanced alternatives.

Practical Applications In Stress Management

Cognitive restructuring is particularly effective in stress management by helping individuals change how they perceive potentially stressful situations. For example, viewing a challenging project as an opportunity to learn rather than a threat can significantly reduce anxiety and improve performance.

Biases and emotional responses often cloud decision-making. Cognitive restructuring helps clear this fog by promoting rational thinking. By reassessing the mental processes that lead to decision-making, individuals can make more considered and objective decisions.

Real-Life Applications

In the Workplace: Cognitive restructuring significantly influences how employees view and handle daily workplace challenges. This technique can dramatically improve the work environment by encouraging a more positive and proactive approach among team members. A key use of this method is in changing how staff respond to feedback. Often, feedback is seen as criticism and can cause defensive or negative reactions. However, cognitive restructuring helps employees learn to see feedback in a positive light.

For instance, a case study at a mid-sized tech company involved workshops that taught team members to think differently about feedback. These workshops included activities where employees practiced changing their immediate negative thoughts about criticism. Rather than taking feedback as a personal attack, they were taught to view it as helpful information that guides their professional growth and improvement. Over time, this new way of thinking led to better teamwork and fewer conflicts during performance reviews. Employees started seeing feedback sessions as opportunities for learning and development, which greatly improved their work relationships and personal growth.

In Personal Relationships: Cognitive restructuring can greatly improve personal relationships by helping people rethink their expectations and interpretations of each other's actions. This approach is often used in marriage counseling to help couples change negative patterns that cause problems in their relationship.

For example, one couple was constantly arguing because they misunderstood each other's actions and intentions. In their therapy sessions, which focused on cognitive restructuring, they learned to recognize and question their immediate negative reactions. For instance, if one partner felt left out when the other was busy with hobbies, they were taught to change their thoughts from "I am being ignored" to "My partner is taking time for themselves, which is good for their well-being and our relationship." This change in perspective helped them see each other's actions in a more positive light, reducing arguments and increasing support for one another.

These real-life applications underline the versatility and effectiveness of cognitive restructuring. By changing how situations are perceived, cognitive restructuring not only enhances workplace dynamics but also deeply enriches personal relationships. It encourages a shift from a defensive, critical perspective to an open, growth-oriented mindset, enabling better communication, reduced conflict, and more productive interactions in various aspects of life.

Tips For Maintaining Cognitive Restructuring Practices

Regular Practice: Like any skill, the benefits of cognitive restructuring are most pronounced with regular practice. It is beneficial to assess and adjust thought patterns routinely.

Journaling: Keeping a thought diary can be an effective way for individuals to track their thoughts and the situations in which negative patterns arise, providing a basis for restructuring.

Professional Guidance: Initially, it may be helpful to work with a therapist who can guide the cognitive restructuring process and provide objective feedback.

Cognitive restructuring is a valuable tool for mental health that helps people overcome negative thinking patterns and become more resilient. By incorporating these techniques into everyday life, individuals can develop a healthier mindset, which leads to better emotional well-being and a higher quality of life. As we move forward in this book, the connection between cognitive techniques and essential life skills will become more apparent, highlighting how mental flexibility is crucial for personal and professional success.

CHAPTER 5: LEARNING TO LEARN

"The first principle is that you must not fool yourself—and you are the easiest person to fool."

— RICHARD FEYNMAN

Learning is a fundamental part of personal and professional growth. The Feynman Technique, named after the physicist Richard Feynman, is a powerful method for understanding and retaining complex information. This chapter explores the principles of the Feynman Technique, its application in various learning scenarios, and its benefits for professional and personal development.

Understanding The Feynman Technique

The Feynman Technique is based on the premise that teaching is the best test of understanding. The method involves four key steps: choosing a concept, teaching it to a novice, identifying gaps in understanding, and reviewing and simplifying the explanation. This technique aids in deeper learning and uncovers and fills knowledge gaps.

The Four Steps

Choose a Concept: Select a topic or concept you want to understand better. It could be anything from a scientific theory to a business model.

Teach It to a Child: Explain the concept as if you are teaching it to a child. Use simple language and avoid jargon. The goal is to make the explanation accessible and understandable at an elementary level.

Identify Gaps in Understanding: During the explanation process, pay attention to points where you struggle to use simple language or skip over complicated parts. These are indicators of gaps in your understanding.

Review and Simplify: Enhance your understanding by refining the explanation. Consult additional resources or texts to address any gaps in your knowledge. Continue revising your explanation until you can articulate the concept in straightforward terms, demonstrating a thorough grasp of the subject.

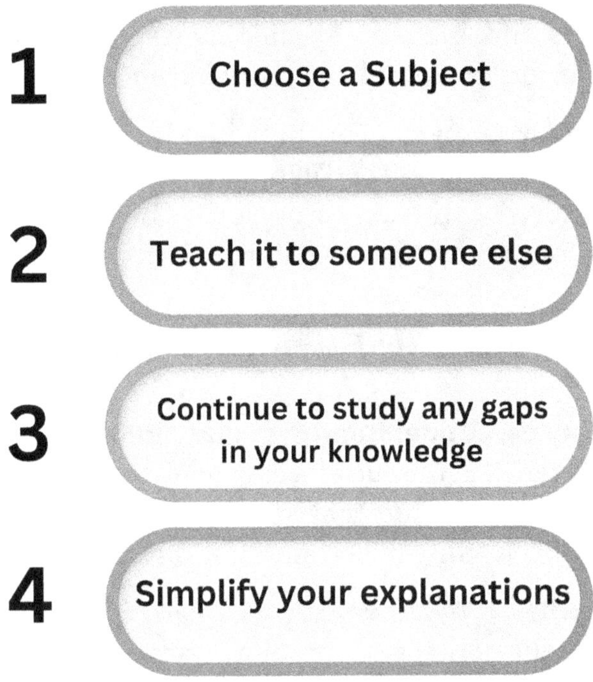

Steps of the Feynman learning technique

Applications Of The Feynman Technique

Education: Students can use this method to grasp complex subjects by breaking them down into simpler components. It proves particularly beneficial for abstract subjects such as mathematics, physics, and philosophy.

Professional Development: This technique can be employed by professionals to master new skills or understand industry-specific concepts, enhancing job performance and career advancement.

Personal Growth: For individuals committed to lifelong learning, the Feynman Technique offers a structured approach to exploring new hobbies or areas of interest with depth and clarity.

Benefits Of The Feynman Technique

Enhanced Understanding and Retention: The Feynman Technique forces you to use simple language, ensuring that you truly understand the material, leading to better retention and recall.

Identifies Weaknesses: Regularly using this technique helps pinpoint areas of weak understanding, which can be targeted for improvement.

Adaptable Learning: This technique is not restricted to any discipline and can be adapted to learn almost anything, enhancing its utility across various contexts.

Practical Exercises Using The Feynman Technique

Daily Learning Journal: Keep a journal where you write down daily learnings or concepts, applying the Feynman Technique to each entry. This reinforces learning and improves your ability to communicate complex ideas.

Study Groups: Organize or join study groups where each member teaches a concept to the group using the Feynman Technique. This collaborative approach can deepen understanding and expose different perspectives on the same topic.

Work Presentations: Use the Feynman Technique to prepare for presentations at work. This will help ensure your audience understands your points clearly, making your presentations more effective.

Challenges And Solutions

Over-Simplification: There's a risk of oversimplifying complex concepts, potentially omitting nuanced details. To counteract this, balance simplicity with depth to maintain accuracy.

Time-Consuming: While effective, the Feynman Technique can be time-consuming. To manage this, apply it selectively to concepts that you find particularly challenging or essential.

The Feynman Technique is more than just a learning method; it is a tool for intellectual discipline and a catalyst for continuous improvement. By adopting this technique, individuals can enhance their capacity to learn effectively, think clearly, and communicate precisely. As we progress through this book, the interconnectedness of practical learning with strategic thinking and decision-making will continue to unfold, showcasing the critical role of the Feynman Technique in fostering a prosperous, lifelong learning journey.

PART III: ADVANCED THINKING AND DECISION MAKING TOOLS

CHAPTER 6: ROOT CAUSE ANALYSIS

"Don't look for faults; find remedies."

-SAKICHI TOYODA

Understanding the underlying causes of problems is crucial for effective problem-solving in any endeavor. The Five Whys technique, a simple yet powerful tool for root cause analysis, offers a straightforward approach to diagnosing the essence of an issue. This chapter explores the Five Whys' origins, methodology, and application in various contexts, emphasizing its role in enhancing decision-making and operational efficiency.

Origins Of The Five Whys

Developed by Sakichi Toyoda and later popularized in the Toyota Production System by Taiichi Ohno, the Five Whys technique was initially used to enhance manufacturing processes. The simplicity of asking "Why?" five times successively is designed to peel away the layers of symptoms to uncover the root cause of a problem.

Principles Of The Five Whys Technique

The core principle behind the Five Whys is that most problems can be traced sequentially to their root cause through an iterative process of asking why they occur. This technique helps distinguish between symptoms and the underlying cause of a problem, which more visible issues can often obscure at the surface.

Step-By-Step Implementation

Identify the Problem: Clearly define the problem you are facing. This step is crucial as the entire analysis is based on this definition.

Ask the First Why: Ask why the problem happens and record the answer. This should be a straightforward statement directly related to the problem.

Follow Up with Four More Whys: Continue asking why the answer to the previous question occurs. Each response should lead naturally to the next question, delving deeper into the issue.

Determine the Root Cause: The answer to the fifth why should reveal the root cause of the initial problem. This is typically a fundamental issue that, when addressed, prevents the initial problem and its symptoms from recurring.

Implement Solutions: Develop and implement strategies or corrective actions to address the root cause. This step ensures that the problem remains.

Applications Across Different Fields

Business Operations: In business, the Five Whys can be used to solve production issues, improve service delivery, and enhance customer satisfaction by addressing systemic problems.

Software Development: In the tech industry, the Five Whys help debug software issues, enhance user experience, and refine systems architecture.

Personal and Professional Development: Individuals can use this technique for personal problem-solving and professional growth, such as career development challenges or workplace conflicts.

Benefits Of The Five Whys

Simplicity and Accessibility: One of the greatest strengths of the Five Whys is its simplicity. It requires no advanced tools or technologies, making it accessible anywhere.

Promotes Deeper Understanding: The Five Whys foster a better understanding of the processes and systems involved by forcing a deeper investigation into problems.

Prevents Problem Recurrence: Addressing the root cause of issues rather than symptoms ensures that the same problems are less likely to recur, saving resources and time in the long run.

Common Pitfalls And How To Avoid Them

Stopping Too Early: One risk of using the Five Whys is stopping before reaching the root cause. It's essential to be diligent and ensure the process is completed on time.

Lack of Diverse Perspectives: Relying on a single perspective can lead to biased or incomplete conclusions. Engaging a diverse group of people in the analysis can provide a more comprehensive understanding of the problem.

Overreliance on Intuition: While intuitive answers can sometimes lead quickly to the root cause, they can also mislead. Supporting each conclusion with data or evidence is crucial.

The Five Whys technique is valuable for anyone

looking to solve problems effectively. From personal life to professional settings, mastering this technique can significantly improve how challenges are approached and resolved. As we explore advanced thinking tools in the following chapters, the foundational skills developed through the Five Whys will be a base for tackling more complex problem-solving scenarios. This technique not only aids in problem resolution but also enhances strategic thinking capabilities, making it indispensable for continuous improvement in various aspects of life and work.

CHAPTER 7: LATERAL THINKING FOR INNOVATIVE SOLUTIONS

"You cannot dig a hole in a different place by digging the same hole deeper."

— EDWARD DE BONO

In a world where conventional solutions often fail to address new challenges, lateral thinking emerges as a crucial skill. This chapter explores the concept of lateral thinking, its role in fostering innovation, and how it differs from traditional problem-solving methods. Practical techniques and real-world examples will illustrate how lateral thinking can lead to breakthrough solutions and transformative innovations.

Understanding Lateral Thinking

Lateral thinking is a creative problem-solving approach that was introduced by Edward de Bono in the 1960s. This method encourages people to look at problems from fresh and unique perspectives rather than using the typical step-by-step logical reasoning. The idea is to think "outside the box" to find innovative solutions that might not be immediately obvious.

This approach involves challenging the usual ways of thinking and exploring more unconventional ideas. For instance, instead of following a linear path to solve a problem, lateral thinking might suggest jumping ahead or looking at seemingly unrelated factors that could influence the situation. This can lead to surprising and creative solutions that traditional logical methods might miss.

By using lateral thinking, individuals can stimulate their imagination and gain deeper insights into the issues at hand. This method helps break down the barriers set by usual reasoning processes, which often confine our thinking to familiar patterns and solutions. Lateral thinking opens up a whole new realm of possibilities, making it a valuable tool for innovation and problem-solving in various fields, from business to education and beyond.

In practice, lateral thinking can be as simple as asking unusual questions that challenge common assumptions, or it might involve more structured exercises like brainstorming sessions where all ideas are considered without immediate judgment. This method not only helps find novel solutions but also enhances the overall creativity of the individuals or teams involved, fostering a more dynamic and flexible approach to challenges.

Lateral Vs. Vertical Thinking

While vertical thinking drives one to proceed with logical, incremental steps, lateral thinking demands disruptive, non-linear jumps. Vertical thinking solves problems predictably; lateral thinking provokes unexpected solutions. For instance, while vertical thinking might optimize an existing path, lateral thinking would question the path's existence or create a new one altogether.

Techniques Of Lateral Thinking

Provocation: Introducing an absurd or illogical statement forces the mind to search for connections or alternatives, sparking creativity. For example, saying "cars should fly" can lead to innovative thinking about transport.

Random Input: Grabbing a random word or picture and associating it with the problem at hand can unblock conventional thinking patterns and lead to novel ideas.

Reversal: Turning the problem or situation upside down can uncover surprising new possibilities and insights.

Challenge Assumptions: Deliberately challenging the basic assumptions on which a problem rests can reveal new pathways to solutions previously obscured by conventional thinking.

Practical Applications In Business And Innovation

Product Development: Companies can use lateral thinking to innovate products by sidestepping traditional design constraints and re-imagining what a product could be or do. Apple's creation of the iPhone, which shifted the focus from keypad-based phones to touch interface, is a prime example of lateral thinking in product innovation.

Business Strategy: Lateral thinking can redefine business strategies by exploring unconventional market positions or novel business models. Netflix's transition from DVD rentals to streaming services disrupted traditional media distribution channels.

Marketing: Creative advertising that captures public

imagination often stems from lateral thinking. The famous "Dove Real Beauty Sketches" campaign redefined beauty advertising by focusing on self-perception versus others' perceptions.

Lateral Thinking In Problem Solving

Real-world problems often benefit from a lateral thinking approach, which can leapfrog over obstacles that resist traditional solutions. For example, addressing urban congestion traditionally focuses on improving road infrastructure; lateral thinking suggests reducing the need for travel through telecommuting policies.

Enhances Creativity: Lateral thinking breaks the shackles of conventional frameworks, improving individual and organizational creativity.

Speeds Up Problem-Solving: Bypassing iterative trials and errors can lead to quicker solutions.

Fosters Innovation: It opens up new avenues for innovation by challenging the status quo and exploring beyond the obvious.

Challenges

Lateral thinking can sometimes lead to ideas that are creative but not always practical or feasible. It is important to carefully evaluate and refine these ideas to ensure they can actually work in real-world situations. Furthermore, when people come up with innovative solutions, they often face resistance from others who are accustomed to traditional ways of thinking. To overcome this, it's essential to foster an environment that welcomes change and encourages people to experiment with new approaches. Additionally, while lateral thinking is valuable for generating unique solutions, it should not completely replace traditional, step-by-step (vertical) thinking. The most effective approach usually combines both lateral and vertical thinking. This combination allows for creativity while also keeping ideas realistic and grounded. Balancing these two methods helps ensure that innovative concepts are both imaginative and practical.

Lateral thinking is not just a tool for creativity—it's a fundamental skill for the 21st century. As industries and societal structures become more complex, thinking outside conventional frameworks becomes increasingly essential. This chapter has laid out both the theoretical framework and practical applications of lateral thinking, providing a roadmap for those looking to harness this powerful approach to innovation. In the subsequent chapters, we will see how these innovative techniques interplay with advanced decision-making tools, further enhancing our ability to tackle complex problems and generate impactful solutions.

CHAPTER 8: ENSURING COMPLETENESS

"Checklists cannot fly airplanes for you, but they can ensure priorities are set and nothing is overlooked at critical junctures."

— DANIEL BOORMAN

In high-stakes environments, ensuring that nothing is overlooked is paramount. "The Checklist Manifesto," inspired by Atul Gawande's book advocating for checklists in medicine, explores how this simple tool can dramatically improve accuracy and reliability across various fields. You will learn the importance of checklists, the steps for creating effective and reliable ones, and real-world examples of successful checklist implementation.

The Importance Of Checklists

Checklists are powerful tools that offer a simple yet effective way to ensure that all necessary steps in a process are completed. By explicitly listing actions that need to be taken, checklists can prevent errors and oversights caused by memory lapses, attention failures, or lack of knowledge. They are especially crucial in complex environments where the cost of mistakes is high, such as in aviation, healthcare, and project management.

Creating Effective Checklists

Identify the Processes: Begin by mapping out the processes or tasks that need a checklist. Focus on areas where mistakes occur frequently or where the consequences of errors are severe.

Define Clear, Concise Tasks: Each item on the checklist should be a specific action that needs to be performed. Avoid ambiguity to ensure that anyone using the checklist understands precisely what is required.

Organize Logically: Arrange the tasks in the order they need to be completed. Group related tasks together to make the checklist easier to follow during execution.

Test and Refine: Before finalizing a checklist, it should be tested in the real-world environment where it will be used. This testing phase is crucial to identify any items that might have been overlooked or steps that need clarification.

Keep It Short and Practical: The best checklists are concise and to the point. They should be manageable and detailed, as too much can make them cumbersome and reduce compliance.

Successful Examples Of Checklist Implementation

Healthcare: In surgical settings, checklists have significantly reduced the rates of infection and surgical complications. They ensure that all standard safety protocols are followed, such as confirming patient identity and the surgical site.

Aviation: Pilots use pre-flight checklists to verify that all systems are functional before takeoff. This practice has made commercial flying one of the safest modes of transportation.

Project Management: Checklists in project management can help track project milestones and deliverables, ensuring that all project requirements are met and communicated clearly among team members.

Real Estate Agents: House closing have many steps,

from inspections, to dealing with title agents or lawyers and making sure utilities are switched. Checklists make sure nothing is missed and a home sale goes smoothly.

Benefits Of Using Checklists

Reduces Errors: By providing a standard procedure for tasks, checklists lessen the likelihood of skipping steps or making errors.

Increases Efficiency: Checklists can speed up the process by eliminating the need to remember every step, allowing more mental space for focusing on task execution.

Improves Consistency: When checklists are used regularly, they ensure that tasks are completed consistently, regardless of who performs them.

Enhances Team Communication: Checklists serve as communication tools that help synchronize team activities, ensuring everyone is aligned with their roles and responsibilities.

Challenges And Solutions

Resistance to Adoption: Some professionals may view checklists as bureaucratic or an implication that they need to be more skilled to remember their tasks. Overcoming this requires demonstrating the benefits of checklists through case studies and pilot programs.

Over-Reliance on Checklists: While checklists are helpful, they are not a substitute for professional judgment. Training and guidelines should emphasize that checklists are tools to enhance, not replace, expertise.

Maintaining Relevance: Checklists must be regularly reviewed and updated to adapt to new information or procedure changes. This requires a commitment to continuous improvement.

Checklists are a testament to the power of simplicity in achieving reliability and efficiency. They offer a systematic approach to ensuring that everything is noticed in complex procedures, thus enhancing outcomes and reducing errors. As we explore other decision-making and problem-solving tools in the subsequent chapters, the foundational principles provided by practical checklist usage will recur as a theme, underscoring the importance of systematic approaches in achieving precision and excellence in any field.

CHAPTER 9: MANAGING MENTAL RESOURCES

— JOHN TIERNEY

Decision fatigue refers to the deteriorating quality of decisions an individual makes after a lengthy decision-making session. It manifests when the mind, burdened by constant decision-making, begins to look for shortcuts, either by making hasty decisions or avoiding decision-making altogether. This phenomenon can lead to poor judgment and ineffective outcomes, affecting not just daily choices but also significant life decisions that can impact academic and professional performance, increase stress levels, and decrease the overall quality of life.

Psychological Impact And Symptoms

The psychological toll of decision fatigue is profound. Individuals may experience increased procrastination as they delay decisions to avoid mental strain. Impulsivity may also rise, with snap decisions made without considering the consequences. In some cases, there is a marked avoidance of decision-making, with some delegating decisions to others to escape the burden. A notable symptom is reduced regulation, where individuals struggle to resist temptations or stick to planned actions.

Procrastination: Delaying decisions to avoid the mental strain of decision-making.

Impulsivity: Making hasty decisions without fully considering the consequences.

Avoidance: Skipping or delegating decisions to others.

Reduction in self-regulation: Failing to resist temptations or stick to planned courses of action.

Strategies For Managing Decision Fatigue

To combat decision fatigue, simplifying daily choices can significantly conserve mental energy. This involves establishing routines that automate decisions or reducing the range of options in daily tasks. Prioritizing decisions is crucial; it is most effective to handle important decisions first thing in the morning when mental energy is at its peak. Implementing structured routines can reduce the number of decisions one has to make, thereby conserving mental energy for important tasks. Regular breaks throughout the day are vital as they help replenish mental stamina, maintain a sharper focus, and improve decision-making capacity. Maintaining optimal nutrition and ensuring adequate sleep support cognitive functions and decision-making abilities.

Simplify Choices: Reducing the number of decisions needed each day can help preserve mental energy. This can be achieved by establishing routines or limiting options in daily tasks.

Prioritize Decisions: Make the most important decisions at the beginning of the day when your mental energy is at its peak. This helps ensure that critical decisions are made with a fresh mind.

Implement Routine Structures: Routines reduce the need for decision-making by automating daily choices. Steve Jobs famously wore the same outfit every day to eliminate small, energy-consuming decisions.

Take Scheduled Breaks: Regular breaks replenish mental energy. Techniques like the Pomodoro Technique, which involves taking a five-minute break every 25 minutes, can help maintain focus and decision-making clarity throughout the day.

Optimize Nutrition and Sleep: Proper nutrition and adequate sleep are essential for optimal brain function. A well-rested and nourished brain is better equipped to handle the demands of frequent decision-making.

Real-World High-Stakes Decisions

In high-pressure professions like healthcare, decision fatigue can affect the quality of decisions made by doctors, who often perform better at the start of their shifts. The judiciary system shows similar patterns, with judges giving less favorable rulings later in the day. In corporate environments, executives facing long meetings may lose their decision-making capacity as fatigue sets in. To manage high-stakes decisions when tired, delegating less critical decisions, using decision aids like checklists, and engaging in mindfulness practices can be effective strategies. These approaches help maintain decision-making clarity even under duress.

Challenges And Solutions

Addressing decision fatigue is challenging due to cultural and professional norms that often value long working hours and high productivity, sometimes at the cost of mental well-being. Changing these ingrained norms requires a systemic organizational commitment to recognizing and mitigating mental strain. On a personal level, changing habits related to sleep and diet requires consistent effort but is crucial for reducing the impacts of decision fatigue.

Recognizing and mitigating decision fatigue is essential for maintaining practical decision-making abilities and overall productivity. By understanding its effects and implementing strategies to manage mental resources, individuals can enhance their capacity to make thoughtful decisions, improving their professional performance and personal life quality. As strategic thinking and efficient problem-solving are crucial in various life aspects, managing decision fatigue effectively is paramount.

CHAPTER 10: SHARPENING CRITICAL THINKING THROUGH QUESTIONS

The Socratic Method is named after the classical Greek philosopher Socrates and involves a conversational technique where people ask and answer questions to stimulate critical thinking and draw out ideas and underlying presumptions. This method is used to deepen understanding and enhance critical thinking skills by encouraging thorough exploration and questioning of topics discussed.

Understanding The Socratic Method

Socrates developed this method on the premise that by asking a series of probing questions, people could determine the accuracy of their beliefs and expand their understanding. This interactive questioning process helps sharpen an individual's thinking and promotes a detailed investigation of complex concepts. It's particularly effective in challenging existing assumptions and broadening the perspectives through which various issues can be viewed.

The Socratic Method is not just about asking questions but engaging in a thoughtful dialogue that encourages a deeper analysis of important topics. This method has proven beneficial in educational settings, where it helps students develop their ability to think critically about the material they learn, not just memorizing facts but understanding their broader implications and the reasoning behind them. By continuously encouraging individuals to question and rethink their ideas, the Socratic Method fosters a more informed and reflective approach to learning and discussing various subjects.

Mechanics Of The Socratic Method

At its core, the Socratic Method involves a series of structured questions that guide participants toward a deeper understanding of the subject matter. The questioner, or facilitator, asks probing questions that challenge existing opinions, pushing the participants to reconsider their reasoning and the basis of their knowledge. This method is characterized by a continuous dialogue in which ideas are deconstructed and reconstructed through thoughtful inquiry.

Implementation In Educational Environments

The Socratic Method is utilized in educational settings to develop critical thinking skills among students. Teachers act as facilitators who ask questions and encourage students to think deeply about the subject. This method is particularly effective in humanities subjects like literature and philosophy, where interpretation and analysis are essential. However, its principles are equally applicable in sciences, where understanding and innovation rely on questioning conventional wisdom.

Use In Professional Development

Beyond the classroom, the Socratic Method is invaluable in professional development, especially in fields that require strong analytical and decision-making skills. In legal education, for instance, the Socratic Method is a staple used to enhance the analytical skills of law students. In business, it can help professionals refine strategies and improve decision-making processes by challenging the status quo and encouraging innovative thinking.

Advantages Of The Socratic Method

Encourages Deep Understanding: By continuously asking "why," the Socratic Method pushes individuals to look beyond surface-level answers and develop a more profound understanding of the issues.

Improves Critical Thinking Skills: This method trains participants to think critically and analytically, which are crucial skills across all disciplines and professions.

Promotes Active Learning: The interactive nature of the Socratic dialogue fosters an active learning environment in which participants are not passive recipients of information but actively engaged in the learning process.

Fosters Self-Reflection: Socratic questioning's reflective aspect encourages individuals to examine their beliefs, values, and knowledge.

Challenges And Effective Strategies

Despite its benefits, implementing the Socratic Method can be challenging, particularly in environments where participants are accustomed to more passive forms of learning. Some may find the method aggressive or intimidating. To mitigate these challenges, facilitators must create a supportive environment that encourages open and respectful dialogue. Setting clear expectations and building a culture of inquiry are essential for effectively using this method.

The success of the Socratic Method depends mainly on the facilitator's skill in crafting open-ended questions that are sufficiently specific to advance understanding. Facilitators must also be adept at managing the discussion to keep it focused while allowing enough flexibility for exploratory thought.

The Socratic Method remains a powerful educational tool and professional development technique that challenges conventional thinking and fosters a deeper, more reflective understanding. Through systematic questioning, individuals develop the ability to think critically and engage more deeply with the material, an increasingly important skill in a complex, fast-changing world. As this book progresses, the relevance of the Socratic Method to modern challenges in decision-making, problem-solving, and creative innovation will continue to be highlighted, underscoring its enduring value across various domains.

PART IV: STRATEGIC HABITS AND EFFICIENCY MAXIMIZATION

CHAPTER 11: BUILDING PRODUCTIVE ROUTINES

"We are what we repeatedly do. Excellence, then, is not an act, but a habit."

— ARISTOTLE

Habits' subtle yet profound impact on our daily lives cannot be overstated. Whether good or bad, habits form the underlying patterns that drive our behaviors and, ultimately, shape our lives. This chapter explores the neuroscience behind habits, how they are formed and modified, and their role in enhancing productivity and achieving long-term success.

Understanding Habits

Habits are routines of behavior that are repeated regularly and tend to occur subconsciously. Charles Duhigg, in his book The Power of Habit, describes habits as loops that involve three elements: a cue, a routine, and a reward. Understanding these components can help identify why habits exist and how they can be changed. The cue triggers a behavior, the routine is the behavior itself, and the reward is the benefit associated with the behavior.

From a neurological perspective, habits form through "chunking," which is the brain's way of converting a sequence of actions into an automatic routine. This is seen in the basal ganglia, a brain area crucial for developing emotions, memories, and pattern recognition. Forming habits saves brain effort, so we can perform complex tasks like driving while focusing our conscious minds on other things. However, this efficiency can be a double-edged sword when breaking bad habits.

Creating Productive Habits

Creating new, productive habits involves identifying precise behaviors that lead to the desired outcomes and establishing routines that make these behaviors automatic. This process typically involves:

Identifying Cues: Determine what triggers the current habit and define clear triggers for new habits.

Developing New Routines: Replace old routines with new ones that lead to the desired outcome.

Reinforcing with Rewards: Ensure the new routine is associated with a rewarding experience, reinforcing the habit loop.

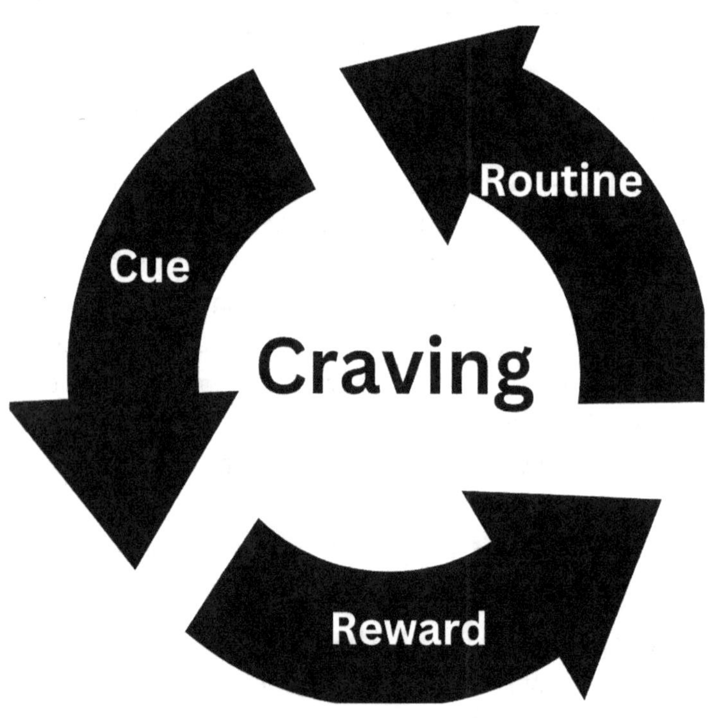

The Habit Loop

Modifying Existing Habits

Modifying an existing habit is about changing the routine rather than eliminating the cue or reward. For example, if stress triggers the habit of eating junk food (cue), replacing junk food with a healthier snack (new routine) can satisfy the same need for comfort (reward) without the negative consequences of the old habit.

Impact On Productivity And Personal Development

Habits powerfully influence productivity. Good habits, such as prioritizing tasks each morning or reviewing performance each evening, can significantly boost efficiency and effectiveness. Personal development habits like regular reading, thoughtful reflection, and consistent exercise contribute to ongoing personal growth and well-being.

Strategies For Sustaining Habits

Sustaining new habits requires more than initial enthusiasm. Key strategies include:

Setting Specific Goals: Clear goals provide direction and help measure progress.

Using Reminders and Notifications: Technology can support habits through reminders that help keep the routines on track.

Social Support: Sharing goals with friends or colleagues can provide encouragement and accountability.

Tracking Progress: Monitoring behaviors helps reinforce the habit loop and motivates visible progress.

Challenges In Habit Formation

Forming new habits often involves overcoming ingrained patterns and resistance to change. Challenges include lapses in motivation, the influence of a hostile environment, and underestimating the time and effort required to make a habit stick. Overcoming these challenges often requires persistence, patience, and, sometimes, strategic adjustments to the planned routines.

Understanding and leveraging the power of habits is fundamental to enhancing productivity and fostering long-term success in both personal and professional domains. By methodically forming and sustaining beneficial habits, individuals can significantly influence the trajectory of their lives, turning productive behaviors into automatic actions that consistently lead to success and fulfillment. As we explore further in subsequent chapters, integrating effective habits with broader strategic plans and goals creates a robust framework for achieving peak performance and maintaining competitive advantage.

CHAPTER 12: FOCUSING ON WHAT MATTERS

"You can do anything, but not everything."

— DAVID ALLEN

The Pareto Principle, commonly known as the 80/20 rule, is a simple yet powerful concept that profoundly impacts efficiency and effectiveness across both personal and professional realms. Whether you're trying to optimize your business operations, streamline workflows, or even improve your personal productivity and time management, the Pareto Principle offers a straightforward approach to identifying the most impactful areas of your work or life. By focusing on these critical tasks or problems, you can achieve more with less effort, enhance your performance, and maximize the outcomes of your endeavors.

Understanding The Origins Of The Pareto Principle

The concept was named after Vilfredo Pareto, an Italian economist who made a striking observation in 1906: 80% of Italy's land was owned by just 20% of its population. Pareto found that this uneven distribution was not unique to land ownership or Italy; it appeared to be a common pattern in various other systems and situations. This led to the formulation of the Pareto Principle, which suggests that in many cases, a relatively small set of factors (about 20%) is responsible for a large portion (about 80%) of the outcome.

This principle has since been recognized as a universal truth in many areas beyond economics, including business management, software engineering, health care, and more. It helps people and organizations identify the most important factors that cause the majority of the problems or results, allowing them to focus their efforts more strategically to maximize efficiency and effectiveness. Whether it's addressing the key sources of revenue in a business or identifying the major causes of a problem, applying the Pareto Principle can lead to significant improvements in how projects and processes are managed.

The 80/20 Rule Across Different Fields

The Pareto Principle is often used in business to maximize productivity and profits. For example, it is commonly observed that 80% of sales come from 20% of clients or that 80% of complaints are generated by 20% of customers. Understanding that 20% of the work often contributes to 80% of the project's value can lead to more focused and efficient project management efforts.

Applications In Personal Productivity

On a personal level, the Pareto Principle can be applied to manage time and resources more effectively. By identifying and focusing on the 20% of tasks that contribute to 80% of one's productivity, individuals can optimize their efforts to achieve better results with less effort. This can apply to daily tasks, career development, and personal relationships.

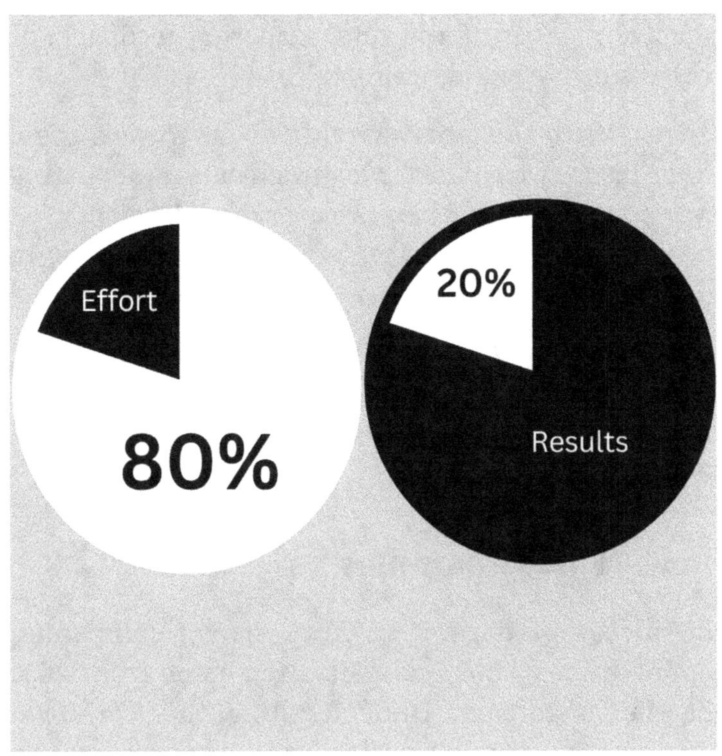

Implementing The Pareto Principle

Identification: The first step is to identify the key inputs or activities that are most productive. This requires tracking and analyzing where time, effort, and resources are currently spent.

Analysis: Once these critical areas are identified, analyze them to understand how they contribute to larger goals or outcomes. This might involve measuring outputs, gathering feedback, or reviewing performance metrics.

Focus: With this analysis, shift focus toward these high-impact activities. This might mean allocating more resources to these areas, scheduling them at peak productivity times, or prioritizing them in daily workflows.

Optimization: Continuously refine and optimize these essential activities. Look for ways to streamline processes, eliminate unnecessary steps, and improve quality.

Real-World Examples

Business Management: In many companies, approximately 80% of sales often come from 20% of the customers. Understanding this can help businesses focus their efforts and resources on the key customers that generate the most revenue.

Software Development: In the realm of software engineering, it's commonly observed that 80% of errors and bugs can be attributed to 20% of the code. Prioritizing efforts on this critical 20% can significantly improve the quality and stability of software.

Healthcare: Within healthcare settings, roughly 80% of healthcare resources are used by 20% of patients. These are typically those with chronic conditions requiring ongoing treatment or management, influencing how healthcare providers allocate resources and manage patient care.

Customer Support: In customer service, 80% of complaints or issues are often caused by 20% of the problems or defects related to a product or service. Identifying and addressing these key issues can greatly enhance customer satisfaction.

Personal Productivity: For many individuals, 80% of productivity may come from 20% of the tasks they perform. Recognizing these high-impact tasks can lead to more efficient time management and greater overall effectiveness in both personal and professional life.

Challenges In Applying The 80/20 Rule

While the Pareto Principle is a powerful tool, its application is challenging. Misidentifying which 20% of efforts lead to 80% of results can lead to wasted resources and opportunities. Additionally, the dynamic nature of business and personal life means that the 20% can change over time, requiring ongoing reassessment and adjustment.

Sustaining The 80/20 Rule

To sustain the benefits of the Pareto principle, it is essential to maintain a cycle of reviewing and recalibrating efforts based on outcomes. This might involve regular reviews of business metrics, personal productivity, or even the health of relationships. Tools such as time-tracking software or feedback mechanisms can aid in continuous improvement.

The Pareto Principle offers a lens through which individuals and organizations can view their work and life to concentrate on what truly matters. Identifying and focusing on the vital few makes it possible to achieve much more with less effort. As we explore efficiency and productivity in subsequent chapters, integrating the Pareto Principle with other management and personal productivity strategies will underscore its relevance and power in achieving peak performance and strategic success.

CHAPTER 13: SEEING THE BIGGER PICTURE

"A system is a network of interdependent components that work together to try to accomplish the aim of the system."

— W. EDWARDS DEMING

Systems thinking is a method of problem-solving that treats problems as parts of a broader system, rather than isolated issues. This approach helps in understanding the big picture and addressing problems more effectively. We will explore the concept of systems thinking, emphasizing its value in managing complex systems and exploring techniques to implement this thinking in both professional and personal scenarios.

Understanding Systems Thinking

Systems thinking is an all-encompassing approach that examines how different parts of a system interconnect and how these connections influence the system over time and within larger contexts. This approach is especially useful in complex environments where numerous subsystems and components interact in detailed and sometimes unexpected ways. The philosophy of systems thinking suggests that addressing individual parts of a problem separately can sometimes lead to unintended consequences elsewhere. Therefore, it emphasizes the necessity of looking at the entire system to find effective solutions. By understanding how various elements influence one another within a whole system, we can predict and mitigate potential problems before they escalate.

Origins And Development

The origins of systems thinking trace back to fields such as biology, engineering, and cybernetics, where understanding interactions and interdependencies within complex systems is crucial. Over time, the concept evolved and began to influence organizational theory and behavior. One of the leading figures in the development of systems thinking was Jay Forrester at MIT, who applied these principles to organizational and social systems. His work led to the creation of methodologies that have provided deeper insights into economic and societal issues through a systemic lens. These methodologies have allowed scholars and professionals to view problems and solutions as parts of an interconnected whole, leading to more sustainable and effective strategies in both business practices and policy-making.

By embracing systems thinking, individuals and organizations can develop a clearer understanding of the complex networks within which they operate, allowing for more strategic planning and decision-making. This holistic view is crucial in today's interconnected world, where actions taken in one area can have significant ripple effects throughout an entire system.

Principles Of Systems Thinking

Interconnectivity and Interdependence: All system parts are interconnected, and changes to one part affect the other.

Feedback Loops: Systems often have complex chains of cause and effect with feedback loops. Positive feedback loops can lead to exponential growth or decline, while negative feedback loops aim to bring the system into balance.

Causality: Systems thinking involves looking

beyond simple cause and effect, understanding that within complex systems, the cause of an issue may be distant in time and space from the impact.

Applying Systems Thinking In Various Domains

Business and Management: Systems thinking can help business leaders understand market dynamics, organizational structures, and employee interactions, leading to better decision-making and strategic planning.

Environmental Policy: In ecological science, systems thinking helps policymakers understand the complex interactions between human activities and natural ecosystems, leading to more sustainable practices.

Healthcare: In healthcare, systems thinking can improve patient care outcomes by considering the entire healthcare delivery system, including treatment processes, patient flow, and administrative operations.

Education: Educators can use systems thinking to design better curricula and learning environments that reflect the interconnected nature of knowledge.

Techniques And Tools For Systems Thinking

Causal Loop Diagrams: These diagrams help visualize the relationships between different system elements and identify feedback loops.

Stock and Flow Diagrams: These represent the accumulations of resources and their inflow and outflow rates, helping to understand the dynamics over time.

Systems Archetypes: Are essentially templates or recurring patterns that can be observed in various organizational and environmental systems. These patterns help us understand common problems and predict issues that might arise in the future. For example, archetypes like "limits to growth" and "tragedy of the commons" provide insights into typical challenges that many systems face.

The "**limits to growth**" archetype is particularly relevant in situations where initial success or growth starts to slow down due to increasing problems that weren't apparent at first. This pattern helps us understand that unchecked growth often leads to constraints—be it resources running low or increased waste and pollution—that eventually stall progress. Recognizing this pattern early can prompt changes in strategy to sustain growth responsibly without hitting those predictable limits.

Similarly, the "**tragedy of the commons**" archetype describes situations where individual users who have open access to a shared resource, such as public land or the atmosphere, act independently according to their own self-interest and contrary to the common good of all users, leading to the depletion of the resource. This archetype teaches the importance of managing shared resources in a way that balances individual needs with the overall sustainability of the resource.

By studying these systems archetypes, we can more effectively diagnose systemic problems in a range of contexts, from business to environmental management. Understanding these patterns allows us to either prevent issues from happening in the first place or manage them more effectively if they do arise. This knowledge is crucial for long-term planning and creating systems that are resilient, sustainable, and capable of thriving in an interconnected world.

Challenges In Implementing Systems Thinking

One of the significant challenges of systems thinking is the complexity of mapping and understanding all the variables and interactions within a system, which can be daunting and time-consuming. Additionally, systems thinking requires a shift in mindset from linear to holistic, which can be difficult for individuals who are used to traditional approaches to problem-solving.

Sustaining Systems Thinking Practices

Organizations and individuals should focus on continual learning and adaptation to effectively implement and sustain systems thinking practices. This includes regular training in systems methods, fostering collaboration and open communication, and employing iterative processes that adjust strategies based on feedback and changing conditions.

Systems thinking offers a robust framework for navigating modern life and work complexities. By understanding the broader systems in which problems reside, individuals and organizations can make more informed decisions that lead to sustainable outcomes. As this book progresses, the value of systems thinking in fostering a comprehensive understanding of complex challenges and crafting practical solutions will be further highlighted, demonstrating its critical role in achieving long-term success and viability.

CHAPTER 14: CREATIVE PROBLEM SOLVING

"Problems cannot be solved by the same level of thinking that created them."

— ALBERT EINSTEIN

Creative problem-solving is a pivotal skill in today's dynamic world, where traditional solutions often fail to address novel challenges. The SCAMPER technique, an acronym for Substitute, Combine, Adapt, Modify, Put to another use, Eliminate, and Rearrange, offers a systematic approach to sparking creativity and innovation. This chapter covers each element of the SCAMPER technique, illustrating how it can enhance creativity in various contexts, from business innovation to everyday problem-solving.

Introduction To Scamper

SCAMPER is a creative thinking technique that serves as a guide for questioning assumptions and exploring new ideas to improve products, services, or processes. This method was developed by Bob Eberle, an educator looking for a structured way to help students think creatively and solve problems effectively.

Eberle introduced SCAMPER as part of his efforts to make creative thinking accessible to everyone, not just people in traditionally "creative" roles like artists or designers. He believed that everyone could be creative by systematically questioning and reimagining how things are done. SCAMPER helps users break down a product or process and consider how each element can be changed to create a new, improved version. This method provides a clear, easy-to-follow framework that encourages looking at the familiar in unfamiliar ways, thereby uncovering hidden opportunities for innovation.

For instance, by applying the "Substitute" aspect of SCAMPER, one might consider what materials or components can be replaced in a product to enhance its functionality or reduce costs. "Combine" might lead to merging two features or products to create a more comprehensive solution. Each part of the SCAMPER acronym pushes the user to think outside the box and challenge existing models, which is essential for progress and innovation.

SCAMPER not only facilitates idea generation but also fosters a proactive approach to problem-solving. By systematically examining different aspects of a product or process with these seven strategies, individuals and teams can uncover potential improvements that would likely remain undiscovered through conventional thinking paths. This tool underscores the importance of creativity in problem-solving and highlights how structured approaches can significantly enhance inventive outcomes.

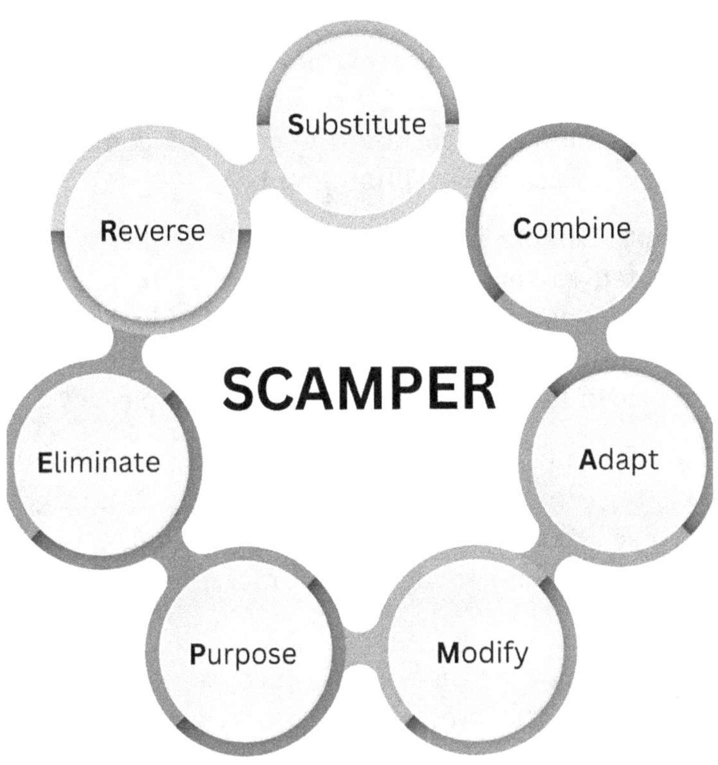

Scamper Components

Substitute: Consider parts of the product or process that could be substituted without altering its core functionality. For instance, replacing sugar with stevia in a recipe can appeal to a health-conscious audience.

Combine: This involves merging two or more project elements to create a new proposition. An example is smartphones incorporating cameras, combining communication with photography.

Adapt: Adaptation asks what elements can be adjusted to serve another purpose or to perform better. Adaptive clothing for individuals with disabilities, which includes magnetic closures instead of buttons, showcases this principle.

Modify: Consider what changes can be made to an existing product or process to improve it. This might involve intensifying or minimizing characteristics, such as making a lighter or more compact tool version.

Put to another use: This encourages thinking about how the product or process could be used differently. Containers used for packaging products can be redesigned for secondary uses by the consumer, reducing waste.

Eliminate: Simplifying the product by removing non-essential parts. This can lead to a more streamlined, cost-effective result.

Rearrange: Look at what would happen if components were rearranged or patterns altered. This could involve changing the sequence of a process to increase efficiency or flipping components to create a new experience.

Applying Scamper In Various Domains

Business Innovation: Companies can use SCAMPER to brainstorm product improvements, service enhancements, or innovative marketing strategies. For example, a furniture company could use SCAMPER to design convertible furniture suitable for smaller living spaces, addressing the trend towards urbanization.

Educational Activities: Educators can use SCAMPER to help students think creatively about projects or in problem-solving scenarios, such as finding new uses for everyday classroom items or rethinking a classic experiment.

Personal Problem Solving: Individuals can apply the SCAMPER technique to everyday problems, such as rearranging home furniture for better functionality or finding new ways to organize personal schedules.

Benefits Of The Scamper Technique

The SCAMPER technique is beneficial because it systematically expands creative possibilities. By methodically exploring these seven strategies, individuals and organizations can uncover solutions that may have yet to be apparent through traditional thinking processes. Moreover, SCAMPER is easy to understand and apply, making it accessible to many users, from professionals to students.

Challenges And Solutions

Implementing SCAMPER can sometimes lead to overwhelming options or impractical solutions. To mitigate this, it's crucial to ground SCAMPER sessions with clear objectives and practical constraints. Additionally, facilitators should guide the brainstorming process to ensure that ideas remain actionable and aligned with strategic goals.

The SCAMPER technique offers a robust framework for unleashing creativity and innovation. Whether used in business, education, or personal contexts, it provides a structured yet flexible approach for rethinking the conventional and discovering new opportunities. As the chapters continue, we will see how integrating the SCAMPER technique with other creative and analytical tools can further enhance problem-solving capabilities and drive innovation in various aspects of life and work.

CHAPTER 15: MASTERING FAST DECISION CYCLES

"Decisions without actions are pointless. Actions without decisions are reckless."

— JOHN BOYD

In dynamic environments where quick decisions are critical, mastering the OODA Loop—Observe, Orient, Decide, Act—can significantly enhance your ability to respond effectively. This decision-making framework, developed by military strategist Colonel John Boyd, was originally designed to outmaneuver opponents in combat by making faster decisions. The concept is crucial for comprehending and reacting more swiftly than competitors or challenging situations in any high-pressure environment.

Understanding The Ooda Loop

The OODA Loop is a decision-making cycle that includes four stages: Observe, Orient, Decide, and Act. It's a method that encourages continuous movement through these stages to keep pace with and adapt to ever-changing situations. Here's a simple breakdown of each component:

Observe: This is the stage where you gather data from the environment. It involves collecting immediate raw information from the surroundings which forms the basis for all subsequent decisions.

Orient: This step involves making sense of the information. You analyze, synthesize, and come to understand the situation based on the observed data. Your background, experiences, and previous knowledge play a significant role in this phase.

Decide: After orienting, you decide the best course of action based on the options available.

Act: Finally, you implement the decision, after which you go back to observing to see the effects of your actions and adjust as necessary.

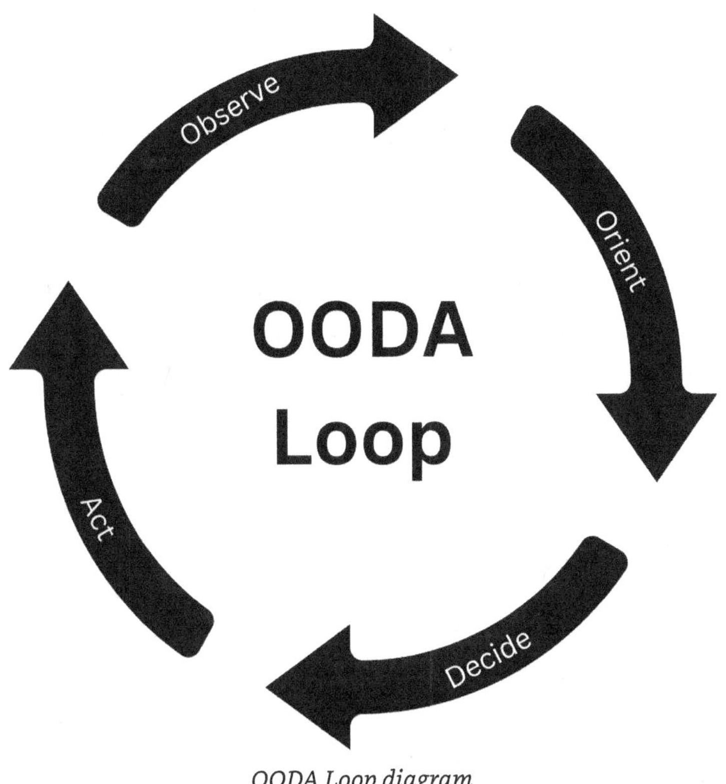

OODA Loop diagram

Initially used in military combat, this framework is now applicable in a variety of fields beyond the military, such as business, sports, emergency response, and everyday personal situations. The ability to quickly move through the OODA Loop can provide significant advantages in any scenario where outcomes depend heavily on speed and adaptability.

For instance, in business, especially in areas like stock trading or crisis management, being able to process information and act faster than competitors can be the difference between substantial gain and loss. In personal situations, such as during an emergency, efficiently cycling through the OODA Loop can help in making quick decisions that could prevent harm. By enhancing your ability to think and act swiftly, you can improve your responsiveness and effectiveness in rapidly changing situations.

Application Across Various Fields

Military and Defense: In combat situations, soldiers use the OODA Loop to assess threats and respond before the enemy can complete their decision cycle, potentially altering the outcome of engagements.

Business and Management: Executives use the OODA Loop to navigate competitive markets, where understanding consumer behavior and technological changes quickly can determine the success or failure of a strategy.

Emergency Services: Rapid observation and quick orientation are crucial for first responders. Decisions must be made swiftly to save lives and mitigate damage during emergencies like fires or natural disasters.

Sports: Athletes and coaches apply the OODA Loop to make split-second decisions that can exploit opponents' weaknesses or respond to their strategies.

Strategies For Mastering The Ooda Loop

Implementing the OODA Loop effectively requires practice and strategic thinking. Here are some strategies to enhance the efficacy of the OODA Loop in decision-making processes:

Enhanced Situational Awareness: Continually updating and expanding the sources of information can improve the observation phase, providing a better foundation for orientation.

Mental Simulation: Regularly practicing scenarios can speed up the orientation phase, as patterns and potential decisions are recognized more quickly.

Decisive Leadership: Encouraging decisiveness in oneself and others streamlines the decision phase, reducing delays that could compromise the effectiveness of actions.

Feedback Loops: Integrating feedback mechanisms into the act phase can inform subsequent observations, ensuring that each loop is more informed than the last.

Challenges And Solutions

One of the main challenges in applying the OODA Loop is cognitive overload, where too much information or too many decisions can stall the process. To combat this, it's essential to enhance data processing capabilities and decision-making skills through training and technology. Additionally, reducing unnecessary complexity in the orientation phase can prevent decision paralysis.

The OODA Loop is more than just a tactical framework; it is a dynamic process that, when mastered, can significantly enhance decision-making speed and effectiveness across various aspects of life and work. Individuals and organizations can maintain a competitive edge in fast-paced environments by continuously cycling through observing, orienting, deciding, and acting. As we continue to explore advanced thinking and decision-making tools, integrating the OODA Loop with other strategies will prove invaluable in navigating complex challenges effectively.

PART V: MINDFUL TECHNOLOGY USE AND REFLECTION

CHAPTER 16: THINKING ABOUT THINKING

"To be conscious that you are ignorant is a great step to knowledge."

— BENJAMIN DISRAELI

Meta-cognition, or "thinking about thinking," is a critical skill that helps individuals understand and manage how they think and learn. We'll explore the concept of meta-cognition, its essential components, strategies to enhance it, its importance in lifelong learning, its use in educational settings, and ways to assess and track meta-cognitive skills.

Understanding Meta-Cognition

Meta-cognition involves two main elements: meta-cognitive knowledge and meta-cognitive regulation. Meta-cognitive knowledge is the understanding of one's own learning processes. This includes knowing which learning strategies work best for oneself and how different factors, like the complexity of the task or how new the information is, can impact learning outcomes. For instance, a student might realize they learn better through visuals rather than through reading, which is an aspect of meta-cognitive knowledge.

Meta-cognitive regulation involves the strategies employed to control one's learning. This includes planning how to tackle a particular task, monitoring one's understanding as the task progresses, and then evaluating the effectiveness of the learning strategy after the task is completed. For example, while working on a complex math problem, a student might periodically check to ensure they understand each step before moving on, and afterward, they might review their approach to see what worked and what didn't.

Historical Context Of Meta-Cognition

The formal study of meta-cognition dates back to the early 20th century but gained significant prominence in the 1970s through the work of psychologist John Flavell, who first coined the term "meta-cognition." Flavell's research brought attention to the ways in which understanding one's cognitive processes could enhance learning outcomes. He distinguished between meta-cognitive knowledge (knowledge about cognitive processes) and meta-cognitive experiences (actual experiences of using those cognitive processes during tasks). This distinction helped shape further research and practical applications in educational psychology, leading to more effective teaching strategies that encourage students to reflect on and manage their learning tactics.

Techniques For Enhancing Meta-Cognitive Awareness

Improving meta-cognitive awareness is critical to becoming a more effective learner. Techniques to enhance this skill include:

Self-Reflection: Regular self-reflection on what one has learned and how one has approached the learning process is crucial. This can be facilitated through journaling or discussing thoughts and strategies with peers or mentors.

Explicit Instruction in Meta-Cognitive Strategies: Teaching students specific strategies for planning, monitoring, and evaluating their learning can improve their meta-cognitive skills. For example, teachers can guide students in setting specific goals, monitoring their understanding of a topic, and adjusting their learning tactics accordingly.

Questioning Techniques: Encouraging learners to ask themselves questions that probe deeper into their learning processes and strategies helps develop meta-cognitive skills. Questions such as "What do I already know about this topic?" or "How can I check if I've understood this correctly?" are helpful.

Think-Alouds: In this technique, individuals verbalize their thoughts while completing a task. This method is often used in educational settings to model how expert learners think through a problem.

Role Of Meta-Cognition In Lifelong Learning And Adaptability

Meta-cognition plays a vital role in lifelong learning and adaptability. By understanding and controlling their learning processes, individuals can adapt to new situations, learn new skills effectively, and respond flexibly to life's challenges. Meta-cognitive skills help learners to be self-directed, able to assess the demands of a task, select appropriate strategies, and adjust their approach based on feedback. This adaptability is crucial not only in formal educational settings but also in the workplace and personal development.

Examples Of Meta-Cognitive Strategies In Educational Settings

Educators can foster meta-cognitive skills through various strategies:

Integrating Meta-Cognitive Prompts: Teachers can integrate prompts into lessons to encourage students to reflect on their learning process. For example, after a science experiment, a teacher might ask students to write about their strategies for conducting the experiment and what they could do differently next time.

Collaborative Learning: Group work can include roles focusing on meta-cognitive strategies, such as a "monitor" who checks if the group's work aligns with the assignment requirements.

Case Studies: Analyzing case studies allows students to practice meta-cognitive strategies by thinking about how they would resolve complex real-world problems.

Measuring And Tracking Improvements In Meta-Cognitive Skills

Measuring and tracking meta-cognitive skills can be challenging due to their intangible nature. However, several approaches can be practical:

Self-Report Questionnaires: Tools like the Meta-cognitive Awareness Inventory (MAI) allow individuals to self-assess their meta-cognitive awareness.

Observational Methods: Teachers or peers can observe and note the use of meta-cognitive strategies during learning activities.

Performance Assessments: Tasks that require meta-cognitive strategies can measure how well these skills are being applied. Performance improvements over time indicate growth in meta-cognitive skills.

Reflective Writing: Essays or reports that require students to reflect on their learning process can provide insights into their meta-cognitive development.

Meta-cognition is a powerful tool for enhancing personal and professional growth. By fostering an awareness of one's learning processes and the ability to control them effectively, individuals can improve their efficiency and adaptability across various tasks and settings. As learners of all ages increasingly require the skills to adapt to rapidly changing environments, the importance of meta-cognitive skills continues to grow. This chapter has outlined the fundamental aspects of meta-cognition and offered practical advice for developing and measuring these essential skills, laying the groundwork for success in lifelong learning endeavors.

CHAPTER 17: REDUCING COGNITIVE LOAD

"Almost everything will work again if you unplug it for a few minutes, including you."

— ANNE LAMOTT

In the digital age, the constant connectivity offered by smartphones, computers, and other devices can significantly strain mental health and productivity. This chapter covers the impact of digital overuse, provides a step-by-step guide for conducting an effective digital detox, and discusses the benefits of regular disconnection. It also presents case studies to illustrate the positive effects of digital detoxes and offers tips for maintaining a balanced approach to digital consumption.

Impact Of Constant Digital Connectivity

The perpetual access to digital information and social interaction has fundamentally changed how individuals consume media and interact with others. While this connectivity has numerous benefits, it also imposes a significant cognitive load. Constant notifications, the pressure to respond quickly, and the vast amount of information available can lead to mental fatigue, reduced attention spans, and heightened stress. Furthermore, overuse of digital devices, mainly social media, can negatively impact mental health, contributing to feelings of inadequacy, anxiety, and depression.

Conducting An Effective Digital Detox: A Step-By-Step Guide

Recognize the Need: Acknowledge feelings of overwhelm or fatigue associated with digital use. Monitoring screen time through built-in apps or third-party tools can quantify the extent of digital use.

Set Clear Goals: Define what you aim to achieve through a digital detox. Goals include reducing screen time, improving sleep, or enhancing face-to-face interactions with friends and family.

Plan the Detox: Decide on the duration and scope of your detox. This might range from a few hours each day without devices to a week-long break from all non-essential digital activities.

Prepare for the Detox: Inform friends, family, and colleagues about your detox plan to set expectations regarding your availability. Also, alternative activities, such as reading, outdoor activities, or crafts, should be planned to fill the time usually spent on digital devices.

Implement the Detox: Turn off non-essential notifications, remove apps, or log out of accounts to avoid temptation. Use physical and digital tools, such as keeping devices in another room or using app blockers, to support your detox.

Evaluate and Adjust: After completing the detox, reflect on the experience. What benefits did you notice? What was challenging? Adjust your digital habits based on these reflections to develop a more balanced digital life.

Benefits Of Regular Unplugging

Regularly unplugging from digital devices helps reduce mental clutter and restore attention capacities. It can improve sleep quality, as excessive screen time, primarily before bed, disrupts sleep patterns. Detoxing also enhances real-world relationships and promotes more profound, more meaningful interactions. Moreover, it provides opportunities to engage in hobbies and activities that might otherwise be neglected due to time spent online.

Digital Detoxes In Action

Increasing Productivity in the Workplace In a recent initiative at a corporate office, the management introduced mandatory 'screen-free' hours during the workday. This policy required employees to turn off all digital screens for a set period each day to focus on non-digital tasks or take breaks from intense screen use. The result was a noticeable increase in productivity, as employees reported being able to concentrate better without the constant ping of notifications and emails. Additionally, staff members noted an improvement in job satisfaction. They appreciated these periods during the day when they could engage in deep work or simply enjoy a mental break, which contributed to lower stress levels and higher overall job contentment.

Enhancing Mental Health Among College Students A group of researchers conducted an experiment with college students who agreed to a week-long social media detox—abstaining from platforms such as Facebook, Instagram, and Twitter. The study aimed to observe the effects of reducing social media consumption on mental health. By the end of the week, participants reported significant decreases in their anxiety and depression symptoms. The absence of social media reduced the pressure to constantly check notifications and compare themselves to others, which is a common source of stress and anxiety among young adults. This break from social media helped students focus more on in-person interactions and activities, leading to improved mood and well-being.

These examples underline the potential benefits of digital detoxes in different settings. Whether in a professional environment where uninterrupted focus can enhance productivity and job satisfaction, or among students where reducing social media use can alleviate anxiety and depression, taking regular breaks from digital devices proves to be beneficial. Such detoxes help individuals reclaim their attention, reduce stress, and foster better mental health, demonstrating the importance of managing digital consumption in our increasingly online lives.

Tips For Maintaining Balance In Digital Consumption

Mindful Use of Technology: Consider why and how you use digital devices. Ask yourself if your digital activity is purposeful and if it aligns with your larger life goals.

Establish 'Tech-Free' Zones and Times: Create boundaries around digital device use, such as banning phones from the dinner table or designating the bedroom as a screen-free area to improve sleep quality.

Regular Mini-Detoxes: Incorporate short, regular detoxes into your routine, such as a day each week without social media or turning off notifications on weekends.

Educate Yourself on the Impacts of Digital Use: Understanding the effects of excessive screen time on the brain and body can motivate more disciplined use of technology.

Use Technology to Regulate Technology: Leverage apps and software that help monitor and limit screen time to enforce your digital boundaries.

When effectively implemented, a digital detox can significantly lighten the cognitive load caused by today's always-on digital culture. By understanding the impacts of excessive connectivity and taking proactive steps to manage digital consumption, individuals can preserve their mental health, boost productivity, and enhance overall well-being. This chapter has provided a comprehensive framework for engaging in a digital detox, supported by practical case studies and actionable tips to help maintain a balanced digital lifestyle.

CHAPTER 18: THE ART OF REFLECTION

"We do not learn from experience... we learn from reflecting on experience."

— JOHN DEWEY

Reflection, critically analyzing one's experiences, is a cornerstone of personal growth and continuous learning. The importance of reflection, outlines techniques for effective reflective practice, provides examples of how reflection can improve performance across various fields, explores challenges to maintaining a reflective habit, and suggests tools that can facilitate this process.

Importance Of Reflection In Personal Growth And Learning

Reflection enables individuals to examine their experiences, understand their choices, and decide how to improve or adjust their actions. This reflective process is essential for personal growth, deepening one's understanding, and enhancing one's skills. By reflecting on experiences, individuals can make more informed decisions, increase their self-awareness, and prevent past mistakes from recurring. In educational settings, reflective practice helps students assimilate and apply knowledge to solve practical problems. It facilitates ongoing learning and adaptability in professional contexts, which is crucial to career development and effectiveness.

Techniques For Effective Reflective Practice

Practical reflection requires structure and intent. Some proven techniques include:

Journaling: Keeping a daily or weekly journal where one records experiences and feelings can be a powerful reflection tool. Journaling helps capture insights and trends over time, providing a concrete method for tracking personal growth.

Structured Reviews: Setting aside regular times to review events or projects can foster a habitual reflective practice. These reviews can be structured around specific questions, such as "What went well?", "What didn't go well?" and "What would I do differently next time?"

Guided Reflection: Prompts provided by a mentor or through a structured program can help focus reflection sessions and make them more productive. This is particularly useful in educational and professional development programs where specific learning outcomes are expected.

Peer Groups: Group discussions can provide multiple perspectives on the same experience, enhancing one's reflective insights. Groups offer a social component to reflection, often bringing out nuances that one might not consider in isolation.

Examples Of Reflective Practice Improving Performance

Reflective practice has been shown to improve performance in a variety of fields:

Education: Teachers who engage in regular reflective practice often experience improvements in their teaching methods and classroom management skills, leading to better student outcomes.

Healthcare: Medical professionals who reflect on patient interactions and treatment plans frequently develop better diagnostic skills and patient care strategies.

Business: Executives who reflect on their leadership decisions and team management experiences can enhance their organizational impact and improve company culture.

Sports: Athletes and coaches who analyze game performances and training sessions can identify areas for improvement, enhancing individual and team performances.

Challenges In Maintaining A Reflective Habit

While the benefits of reflective practice are clear, there are several challenges to maintaining a regular habit:

Time Constraints: Many individuals need more time to dedicate to reflective practice. Overcoming this challenge involves prioritizing reflection as a critical personal and professional development component.

Emotional Discomfort: Reflection can sometimes lead to uncomfortable insights, and facing one's shortcomings can be emotionally challenging. Creating a safe, non-judgmental space for reflection can help mitigate this discomfort.

Consistency: Developing a consistent habit requires discipline and motivation, which can wane over time. Setting regular schedules and reminders can help maintain consistency.

Tools And Apps That Aid In Reflective Practice

Several digital tools can facilitate effective reflective practice:

Reflective Journaling Apps: Apps like Day One or Reflectly offer structured formats for journaling, with prompts and reminders to guide daily reflections.

Video Diaries: Tools like Journey and Lumen5 allow users to create video diaries, which can be particularly useful for those who prefer speaking to writing.

Feedback and Analysis Tools: Platforms like 360Learning and SurveyMonkey can gather and analyze feedback from peers, which can be a valuable source of reflective insight.

Mind-mapping software: Tools like XMind or MindMeister can help visualize, organize, and link thoughts, which is beneficial in the reflection process.

Reflective practice is an essential skill for continuous personal and professional growth. By critically analyzing experiences and applying learned lessons, individuals can enhance their abilities and adapt more effectively to future challenges. While maintaining a reflective habit can be challenging, the benefits outweigh the efforts. With the help of structured techniques and digital tools, reflective practice can become an integrated part of one's daily routine, significantly improving performance and well-being.

CONCLUSION: INTEGRATING SYSTEMS FOR A CLEARER MIND

"The true sign of intelligence is not knowledge but imagination."

- ALBERT EINSTEIN

Throughout this book, we've explored a variety of systems and models designed to enhance mental clarity and organizational skills. From mind mapping and the Eisenhower Box to the deeper complexities of meta-cognition and systems thinking, each chapter has provided tools and insights to optimize personal and professional life. As we conclude, let's recap the critical systems discussed, encourage experimentation with these techniques, and reflect on the enduring value of continuous improvement and lifelong learning in mental organization.

Recap Of Key Systems And Models

Mind Mapping: Introduced as a dynamic tool for visually organizing thoughts, mind mapping helps break down complex ideas into manageable and interconnected components. This technique fosters creativity and aids clearer thinking by mirroring the brain's associative pathways.

The Eisenhower Box: This model helps prioritize tasks by distinguishing between what is urgent and important, allowing for more effective time management and decision-making.

Meditative Practices: We discussed how regular meditation and mindfulness exercises can significantly enhance focus and reduce the cognitive load, leading to better mental health and increased productivity.

Cognitive Restructuring: This cognitive-behavioral strategy teaches how to identify and alter negative thought patterns, promoting healthier thinking habits and improving emotional regulation.

The Feynman Technique: This approach to learning by teaching others reinforces understanding and exposes gaps in knowledge, making it a powerful tool for deep learning.

The Five Whys: By repeatedly asking "why" to every problem, this technique drills down to the root cause of a problem, simplifying complex situations and clarifying thought processes.

Lateral Thinking: We explored how to approach problems from new angles, encouraging innovation and creative problem-solving beyond traditional methods.

The Checklist Manifesto: This strategy uses checklists to ensure task consistency and completeness, reducing errors and increasing efficiency.

Decision Fatigue: We discussed strategies to combat decision fatigue, ensuring our mental energy is preserved and utilized throughout the day.

The SCAMPER Technique: This creative thinking tool prompts users to Substitute, Combine, Adapt, Modify, Put to another use, Eliminate, or Rearrange components of a product, service, or strategy to spark innovation.

The OODA Loop: This model enhances rapid decision-making by cycling through Observing, Orienting, Deciding, and Acting, and it is particularly useful in high-stakes environments.

Meta-Cognition: Focusing on 'thinking about thinking,' this advanced strategy enhances self-awareness and self-regulation, optimizing learning and personal development.

Digital Detox: Recognizing the mental clutter created by our digital environments, we explored how periodic disengagement can restore focus and reduce stress.

Each model offers unique benefits and can be adapted to different aspects of life, from simple daily planning to complex professional projects.

Experimentation

As diverse as these systems are, the effectiveness of each will vary depending on individual needs, circumstances, and preferences. I encourage you to experiment with these techniques to discover what works best. Mix and match approaches, combine various tools, and customize the strategies to suit your personal style and goals. The process of finding the right mix is itself a learning experience—one that teaches flexibility, problem-solving, and self-discovery.

Continuous Improvement And Lifelong Learning

The journey toward mental clarity and effective organization is ongoing. As life evolves, so too will your needs and the challenges you face. Embracing a mindset of continuous improvement and lifelong learning is essential. The most successful individuals consistently apply themselves to learning new methods, refining existing skills, and staying open to new ideas. Lifelong learning in a mental organization enhances personal and professional effectiveness and contributes to a more prosperous, more fulfilling life.

As you integrate these systems into your life, remember that the ultimate goal is to increase productivity or efficiency and enhance your overall quality of life. These tools are meant to serve you, to clear your mind for higher pursuits and more profound satisfaction.

Final Thoughts

The path to mastering mental organization is not linear or one-size-fits-all. It requires patience, persistence, and a willingness to adapt. But the rewards are substantial. With a clearer mind, you're better equipped to face the complexities of the modern world, make informed decisions, and pursue your goals confidently and creatively. Thank you for joining me on this journey. May the strategies discussed here serve you well, lighting your path to a clearer, more organized mind.

◆ ◆ ◆

As a small independent publisher, I would love to hear your thoughts. Please leave a review on Amazon. Simply scan THIS QR CODE

Thanks for reading!

PS - If you'd like a free copy of my book on how to clean anything and keep it that way in less than 15 minutes a day, visit KevinWagonfoot.com

www.ingramcontent.com/pod-product-compliance
Lightning Source LLC
Chambersburg PA
CBHW071026250726
48653CB00005B/1728